Looking at Countries

RUSSIA

Jillian Powell

W

FRANKLIN WATTS
LONDON•SYDNEY

First published in 2006 by
Franklin Watts
338 Euston Road
London NW1 3BH

Franklin Watts Australia
Hachette Children's Books
Level 17/207 Kent Street
Sydney NSW 2000

ISBN-10: 0 7496 6885 7
ISBN-13: 978 0 7496 6885 3
Dewey classification: 914.7

Series editor: Sarah Peutrill
Art director: Jonathan Hair
Design: Rita Storey
Cover design: Peter Scoulding
Picture research: Diana Morris

Picture credits: Action Press/Rex Features: 21. AK/Keystone/Rex
Features: 15. Heidi Bradner/Panos: 22. Bernd Ducke/Superbild/A1 Pix:
26b. East News/Rex Features: 11. Christiane Eisler/Still Pictures: 19t.
Pavel Filatov/Alamy: 7b. Sylvain Grandadam/Robert Harding
PL/Alamy: 13, 23b. Kainulainen/Rex Features: 17t. Jacques
Langevin/Sygma/Corbis: 1, 9. Gerd Ludwig/Visum/Panos: 17c, 23t.
Buddy Mays/Corbis: 18b. Gideon Mendel/Corbis: 12. Mark
Newman/Lonely Planet Images: 6. Oleg Prikhodko: 7t,18t,19b, 20, 26t,
27. H.Saukkomaa/Rex Features: 16. Sipa Press/Rex Features: 14.
Superbild/A1 pix: front cover, 4, 8, 10, 25. Superbild/Incolor/A1 pix: 24.

Every attempt has been made to clear copyright. Should there be any
inadvertent omission please apply to the publisher for rectification.

A CIP catalogue record for this book is available from the British
Library.

Printed in China

Franklin Watts is a division of Hachette Children's Books.

Contents

Where is Russia?

Russia is a huge country that lies in eastern Europe and northern Asia. It is the largest country in the world.

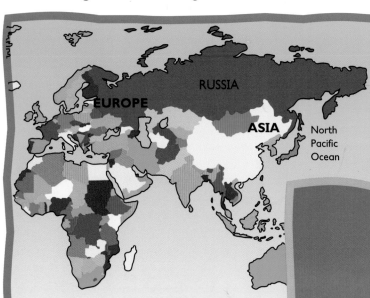

RUSSIA

EUROPE

ASIA

North Pacific Ocean

St. Basil's cathedral in Red Square, Moscow, has nine chapels, each with a colourful 'onion' dome.

Russia's borders stretch from Europe in the west to the North Pacific Ocean in the east.

The capital city, Moscow, is in western Russia. It has many grand buildings and squares including the famous Red Square and the Kremlin.

Russia has a coastline along the Arctic Ocean to the north and the Pacific Ocean to the east. It shares borders with countries in Europe and Asia.

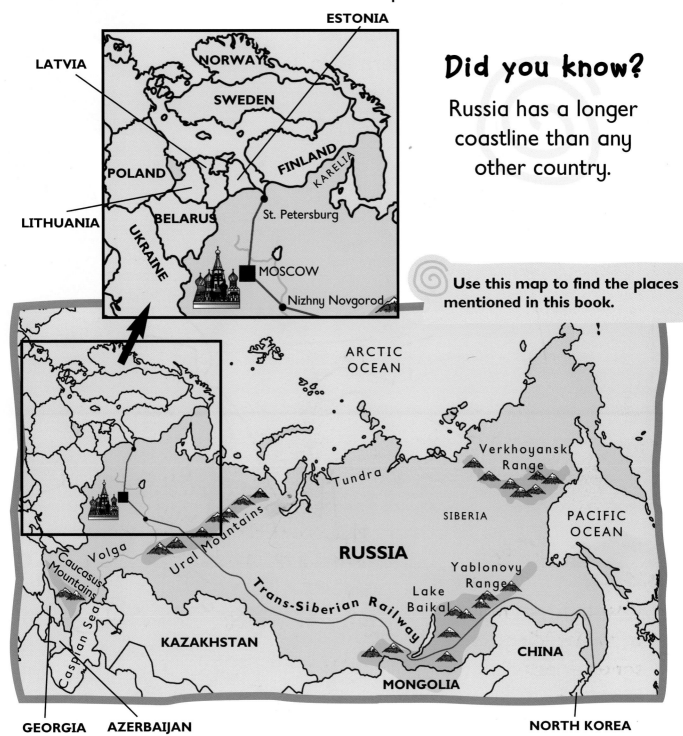

Did you know?

Russia has a longer coastline than any other country.

Use this map to find the places mentioned in this book.

The landscape

In the far north of Russia is the tundra. This is a flat landscape without trees where the soil under the surface is always frozen. South of the tundra, much of northern Russia and Siberia is covered in coniferous forest called taiga.

Did you know?

Russia contains nearly a quarter of the world's woodlands.

Snow and ice melt for a short summer in the tundra.

In central Russia, there are huge areas of plains called steppes.

In the steppes there are no trees. Mostly grasses and low shrubs grow.

The highest mountains are the Urals, which run from north to south between European and Asian Russia, and the Caucasus Mountains in the south-west. Russia also has some of the world's longest rivers, and thousands of lakes including Lake Baikal, the deepest lake in the world.

This snow-capped peak is in the northern Urals.

Weather and seasons

Most of Russia has two main seasons: summer and winter. Everywhere, winters are long and cold, with lots of snow and ice. Rivers and lakes freeze over with temperatures falling to −30°C.

In the south, the summers are short and hot, with the warmest weather in July and August. Most rain falls in the short spring and early summer months.

Most tourists visit the Summer Palace in St. Petersburg in the warmest months, between June and August.

The Nenets people are reindeer herders who live along the Arctic coast, one of the coldest parts of Russia.

The north is cooler than the south. Even the summers are cool along the Arctic coast, and Siberia has a sub-arctic climate, with temperatures falling as low as −70°C in winter.

Did you know?

Russia sometimes has pink or yellow snow — caused by sand and pollution in the air.

Russian people

Over 144 million people live in Russia. Most are Russians, but there are over 100 other ethnic groups including Tatars, Ukrainians and Chuvash. Each has their own language, customs, folk dress and music. Some live in republics that share their government with Russia, but many would like to be independent states.

Did you know?

Russian babies are often named after angels, and children celebrate their angel day as well as their birthday.

This woman is from the Yakut people, who herd cattle and horses in Siberia. She is wearing traditional dress for a festival.

These Russian women are celebrating Christmas. This is one of the most important Christian festivals in Russia.

People also practise different religions. Most Russians are Christians and belong to the Russian Orthodox Church or are Roman Catholics. There are also many Muslims and Jews.

School and home

Russian children must start school when they are six. Many children with working parents start pre-school earlier. The school day starts at 8 am and finishes at lunchtime for younger children and 3 pm for older children. Children can leave school at 16.

These children are enjoying a break outside their school near Lake Baikal.

This family is using a *samovar*, a Russian tea urn, to boil the water for their tea.

Did you know?

In Russia, children have special pies rather than cakes on their birthday.

Most Russians have small families with only one or two children. Grandparents often live with the family and help with the housework and childcare.

Country

About a quarter of the Russian people live in the country. They include many different peoples like the Tatars, the Chuvash and the Yakut. In the north, people herd reindeer and hunt and fish. In the east, they herd cattle and horses.

This girl has been hand-picking a cotton crop.

These herbs have been grown in a greenhouse to protect them from Russia's cold weather.

The biggest farms are in western Russia. Farmers grow crops, such as wheat and barley, or keep cattle, sheep or pigs. Sunflower seeds, sugar beet, cotton and tea are also grown. Fruit and vegetables are grown in the warmer south and in greenhouses in the colder north-east.

In the taiga, many people work in forestry or in the timber and paper-making industries.

Did you know?

Hamsters live in the wild in Russia in the grassy steppes region.

City

Most Russian people live in cities. The largest cities are Moscow and St. Petersburg.

Did you know?

Over 10 million people live in Moscow – the largest city in Europe.

These tower blocks by the river in Moscow were the tallest in Europe when they were built in the 1950s.

Moscow has government offices, banks, theatres, museums and busy shops and restaurants. Many streets have kiosks selling sweets, drinks, biscuits and magazines.

These people are walking in the formal gardens of St. Catherine's Palace in St. Petersburg.

Moscow and St. Petersburg have old buildings and grand squares which sit beside modern tower blocks containing offices or flats.

This is the main shopping street in St. Petersburg.

Many larger Russian cities have public transport including trams, trolleybuses and trains. Moscow, St. Petersburg and Nizhny Novgorod have underground trains to get people around easily.

Russian homes

Most Russians live in blocks of flats in the suburbs of towns and cities. Flats are usually small. Richer families may also own a summer house (*dacha*) in the country where they can spend holidays.

These flats, at the front of the photo, are near to an industrial area.

Many people grow fruit and vegetables for their own use at their *dacha*.

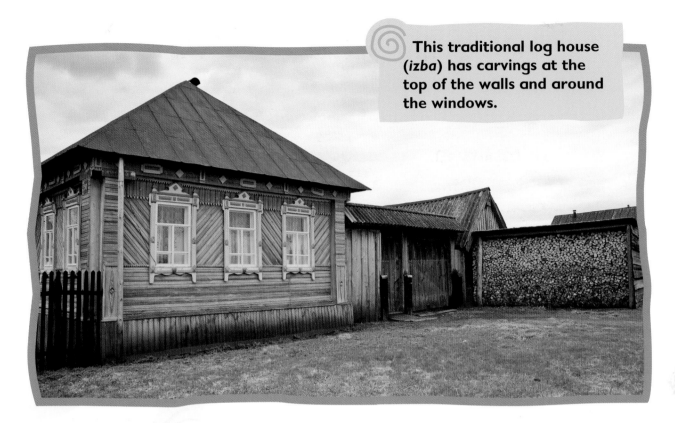

This traditional log house (*izba*) has carvings at the top of the walls and around the windows.

In the country, older houses are made of wood. Traditional log houses (*izbas*) were built in villages around a church or chapel. Each house was different and had decorations carved around doors and windows. Many *izbas* are over 300 years old.

Did you know?

In Siberia, some people live in portable tent homes (*yurta*).

This colourful carved window frame decorates an *izba* house in Karelia.

Food

Traditional Russian dishes include *borshch* (beetroot soup), *shchee* (cabbage soup), *pelmeni* (a meat-filled pasta dish) and *blini* (thin pancakes). Main meals are usually fish or meat eaten with potatoes or rice and pickled vegetables such as cabbage or cucumber.

People shop at supermarkets, small shops and markets for fresh foods such as fish and meat.

In Russia, it is traditional to greet guests with bread and salt.

Fast-food restaurants are popular in Russian cities, especially among young people.

There are Chinese, French, Italian and Japanese restaurants as well as those serving traditional Russian dishes. In cities, fast foods such as hamburgers, hot dogs and ice cream are popular. Street kiosks sell snacks including small meat and vegetable pies called *pirozhki* that can be eaten hot or cold.

Did you know?

The Russians have over 100 different potato dishes.

At work

This man is working in a nickel mine in Siberia, an area rich in metals.

The main industries in Russia include mining coal, gas, oil and metals, building ships, aircraft and machinery, and processing chemicals and foods. There are also factories that make textiles and electronic goods.

Most people in Russian cities work in service industries, such as banking and insurance. There are also jobs in schools, hospitals, restaurants and hotels.

Tourism in Russia is growing fast. City tours, Volga River cruises and journeys on the Trans-Siberian Railway are all popular with tourists. They also like to buy traditional Russian craftwork such as wooden dolls and decorative painted boxes and eggs.

Did you know?

The most popular jobs in Russia include sales and computer programming.

This woman is working as a waitress in a restaurant in St. Petersburg.

Having fun

Russians enjoy many sports. In the summer watching football is popular. In the winter, many people enjoy ice hockey and skating, and snow sports such as skiing. Chess is also popular and there are many chess clubs.

In the cities people visit the ballet and theatre.

Russian ballet dancers perform famous ballets such as *Swan Lake* all over the world.

These people are celebrating the Winter Festival with a traditional ring dance in St. Petersburg.

During the Winter Festival, from 25th December to 5th January, Russians celebrate with troika sleigh rides, skating and dancing. There are also competitions for the best ice sculpture.

Did you know?

In Russia, Christmas Day is celebrated on 7th January.

Russia: the facts

• Russia is a republic. It is made up of many cities, regions and 21 smaller republics.

• Russia is the largest country in the world, with an area of about 17 million square kilometres.

The Russian currency is the rouble.

The Russian flag has bands of white, blue and red.

This grand church is in a small village. Some villages in Russia have as many as 30 churches.

• The president is the head of state and leads the government. The Russian parliament is called the State Duma.

• Until 1991, Russia was part of the Soviet Union (USSR) with 14 other countries. Some of these countries now form a group of independent states.

Did you know?

Russia has over 100 national parks and wildlife reserves. These are wild areas that are carefully looked after by the government.

Glossary

Chapel a building or part of one used for worship.

Coniferous evergreen trees that have needles rather than leaves.

Customs ways of doing things that have been passed down over the years.

Ethnic group a group of people who are part of a common culture.

Folk dress the traditional clothes of a people.

Forestry the industry for growing trees for wood.

Head of state a person who is the main representative of a country.

Kremlin the buildings of the Russian government in Moscow.

Muslims people who follow the religious teachings of the Prophet Muhammad (pbuh).

Nickel a kind of metal.

Parliament a place where the laws of a country are made.

Pickled a food kept fresh by storing it in vinegar.

Pollution dirt in the land or air caused by traffic and industry.

Republic a country with no king or queen, where decision-making power is held by the people.

Service industries industries that provide a service rather than manufacturing something.

Sub-arctic the kind of climate or landscape found close to the Arctic region.

Suburbs the area around a city or town.

Textiles woven or knitted cloth.

Tram an electric train that runs on rails along city streets.

Troika sleigh a sledge for carrying people, pulled by three horses.

Trolleybus an electric-powered bus.

Tundra an Arctic region of treeless plains where the soil underneath is always frozen.

Find out more

www.timeforkids.com/TFK/ goplaces [Click Russia]
Children's website with a history timeline, facts and some Russian words and phrases to learn.

www.teacher.scholastic.com/ activities/globaltrek
[Click Russia]
Website focusing on children living in St. Petersburg, with information on their lifestyle.

www.kidsculturecenter.com/ russia/russia.htm
Information on Russian schools, holidays and recipes.

Note to parents and teachers: Every effort has been made by the Publishers to ensure that these websites are suitable for children, that they are of the highest educational value, and that they contain no inappropriate or offensive material. However, because of the nature of the Internet, it is impossible to guarantee that the contents of these sites will not be altered. We strongly advise that Internet access is supervised by a responsible adult.

Some Russian words

The Russian alphabet is different to the English alphabet. About half of the 33 letters look like English letters, others look different. For example:

Russian A is written and sounds like A in the English alphabet

Russian B sounds like a V in English

Russian letter Ф sounds like F in English

English word	Say ...
Good afternoon	dobri dyen
Goodbye	da sveedaneeya
Good morning	dobra-ye ootra
How are you?	kak dye la?
My name is	myenya zavoot
No	nyet
Please	pazhalsta
Sorry!	prasteet-ye
Thank you	spaseeba
Yes	da

My map of Russia

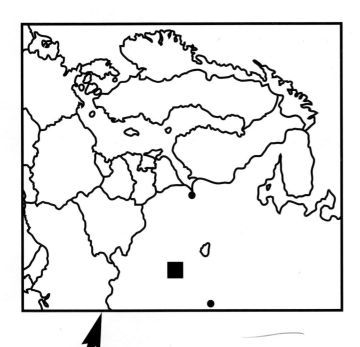

Trace this map,
colour it in and use
the map on page 5
to write the names
of all the places.

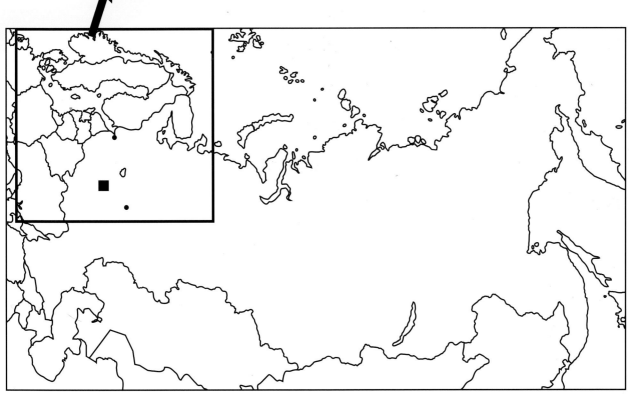

Index